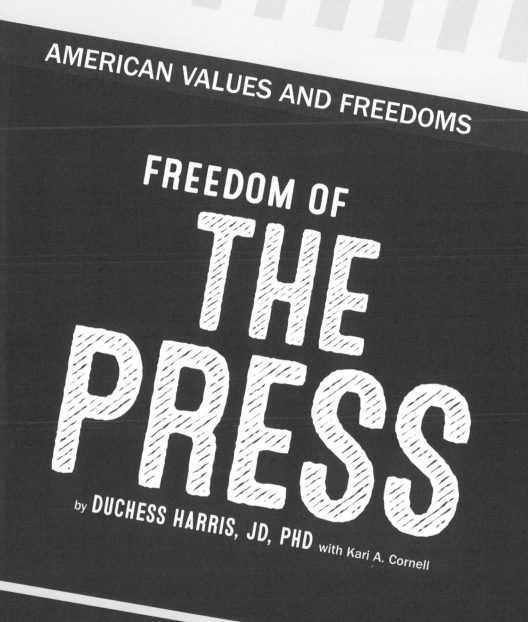

AMERICAN VALUES AND FREEDOMS

FREEDOM OF
THE
PRESS

by DUCHESS HARRIS, JD, PHD with Kari A. Cornell

Essential Library

An Imprint of Abdo Publishing | abdopublishing.com

ABDOPUBLISHING.COM

Published by Abdo Publishing, a division of ABDO, PO Box 398166, Minneapolis, Minnesota 55439. Copyright © 2018 by Abdo Consulting Group, Inc. International copyrights reserved in all countries. No part of this book may be reproduced in any form without written permission from the publisher. Essential Library™ is a trademark and logo of Abdo Publishing.

Printed in the United States of America, North Mankato, Minnesota
102017
012018

Interior Photos: akg-images/Newscom, 4–5; Bettmann/Getty Images, 6, 65; White House Photo Office/Richard Nixon Presidential Library and Museum, 9; JP Laffont/Polaris/Newscom, 11; Eye-Stock/Alamy, 13; Pictures From History/Newscom, 16; Photo Researchers/Science History Images/Alamy, 20; Kentar Cajuan/iStockphoto, 23; GraphicaArtis/Archive Photos/Getty Images, 25; Everett Collection/Newscom, 26; Paul Revere/Library of Congress, 28–29; Everett Historical/Shutterstock Images, 31; H. Devitt Welsh/Library of Congress, 35; FOW/AP Images, 38–39; Godfrey/AP Images, 41; H. Armstrong Roberts/ClassicStock/Alamy, 42; CBS Photo Archive/CBS/Getty Images, 48; Brian PIrwin/iStockphoto, 50–51; Harris & Ewing/Harris & Ewing Collection/Library of Congress, 53; Dorothea Lange NC History Images/Newscom, 54; Jim Wells/AP Images, 56; AP Images, 59; Civil Case Files, compiled 1938 - 1982/U.S. District Court for the Northern (Montgomery) Division of the Middle District of Alabama/The US National Archives, 62; John McCoy UPI Photo Service/Newscom, 69; Kevin Dietsch/UPI/Newscom, 70; Jeff Malet Photography/Newscom, 72; Mario Ruiz/The LIFE Images Collection/Getty Images, 74–75; Mel Evans/AP Images, 77; Shutterstock Images, 80–81; iStockphoto, 84–85; Bill Clark/CQ Roll Call/Newscom, 87; John Angelillo/CNP/Newscom, 90–91; Xinhua/Alamy, 96

Editor: Claire Mathiowetz
Series Designer: Becky Daum

Publisher's Cataloging-in-Publication Data
Names: Harris, Duchess, author. | Cornell, Kari A., author.
Title: Freedom of the press / by Duchess Harris and Kari A. Cornell.
Description: Minneapolis, Minnesota : Abdo Publishing, 2018. | Series:
    American values and freedoms | Online resources and index.
Identifiers: LCCN 2017946725 | ISBN 9781532113000 (lib.bdg.) |
    ISBN 9781532151880 (ebook)
Subjects: LCSH: Freedom of the press–Juvenile literature. | Freedom of the
    press–United States–Juvenile literature. | Censorship–Juvenile literature.
    | Constitutional law–United States–Juvenile literature.
Classification: DDC 323.445–dc23
LC record available at https://lccn.loc.gov/2017946725

CONTENTS

CHAPTER 1

WATERGATE

The first Watergate building opened in 1965. The entire complex is made up of five different buildings, including a hotel.

Early in the morning on June 17, 1972, five men covertly entered the Watergate office building in Washington, DC, and climbed the stairs to the sixth floor. They were looking for the Democratic National Committee (DNC) headquarters. Each of the five men wore a business suit and surgical gloves and carried at least $200 in cash in his pockets.[1] Some carried cameras. Their mission: to photograph key DNC documents related to the upcoming presidential election and install wiretaps into the phone headsets.

But they wouldn't get that far. On a routine check at 1:47 a.m., Watergate security guard Frank Wills noticed that the locks on some of the doors had been taped over. Wills immediately called the police. By 2:30 a.m., the burglars could hear the police storming up the stairs, shouting, "Come out with your hands up!"[2] There was no way out. James W. McCord, Virgilio R. Gonzales, Frank A. Sturgis, Eugenio R. Martinez, and Bernard L. Barker were all arrested and charged with attempted burglary and wiretapping.

NO "THIRD-RATE BURGLARY"

The next day, White House Press Secretary Ronald Zeigler mentioned the incident in his daily briefing. "Certain elements

Bob Woodward, *right*, and Carl Bernstein wrote a book on their experience during the Watergate scandal titled *All the President's Men* that was turned into a movie in 1976.

may try to stretch this beyond what it was," he said, calling it just a "third-rate burglary."[3]

Two investigative reporters for the *Washington Post*, however, thought otherwise. Bob Woodward and Carl Bernstein began looking into the specifics of who was behind the burglary. Their first story on the Watergate break-in identified 53-year-old McCord as the security coordinator for the Republican National Committee and the Committee for the Re-election of the President (CREEP). Other burglars had Central Intelligence Agency (CIA) connections. Clearly there was more to the story than the White House was leading the American public to believe.

PRESS AS GOVERNMENT WATCHDOG

Freedom of the press allows journalists the right and responsibility of reporting the news in a truthful, unbiased way. But more importantly, freedom of the press establishes the media almost as a fourth branch of government, with the role of keeping the government honest. By questioning the government about policies, connecting the dots between related events, and drawing accurate conclusions based on well-documented research, the press provides a check and balance on government policies. The press provides the American people with the information they need to hold leaders accountable.

DIGGING DEEP

With the help of a secret source within the Federal Bureau of Investigation (FBI), whom Bernstein and Woodward called "Deep Throat" to protect his identity, the reporters began to unravel just what happened that night in 1972. The next big break came when they discovered one of the burglars had received a substantial deposit into his bank account—to the tune of $25,000.[4] And the money came directly from President Richard Nixon's campaign fund.

On October 10, 1972, less than a month before the presidential election, Bernstein and Woodward revealed breaking news in the case. The FBI had uncovered critical evidence linking the Nixon reelection committee with the Watergate break-in. It was part of an elaborate campaign to spy on and sabotage the DNC and Democratic presidential candidates.

Although presidential campaigns commonly research the opposition, Nixon's reelection committee went far beyond what is considered standard. In the name of gathering information, members of the reelection committee forged letters and sent them out on the candidate's letterhead. They passed on false stories to the press that reflected on the candidates, and they

NIXON'S DISTRUST

Early in his first term, President Nixon began to resent the media's coverage of the Vietnam War (1955–1975), which pitted the Communist North Vietnam against the non-Communist South. The conflict, which the United States entered in 1965, was not going as planned. By 1971, the drawn-out war had become controversial among the American people, who questioned why US troops were there and when the long war would end. This discontent was fueled by media reports from the front lines, where unlike in any other war, journalists were free to report the war uncensored and as it happened. As the first war to be televised, the grim reality of conditions in Vietnam was projected right into the living rooms of Americans. These reports became fodder for the growing anti-war movement.

Nixon and many others began to blame the press for turning Americans against the war. To stop journalists from leaking information about the war to the public, Nixon had Secretary of State Henry Kissinger arrange for the FBI to bug 17 members of the press. On February 22, 1971, Nixon lamented the problem of the media: "In the short run, it would be so much easier, wouldn't it, to run this war in a dictatorial way, kill all the reporters and carry on the war." Not even a week later, Nixon ordered Admiral Thomas H. Moorer not to trust the press: "The press is your enemy. Enemies. Understand that?"[5]

investigated Democratic campaign workers. They even went as far as to follow family members of Democratic candidates.

NIXON REELECTED

The *Washington Post* published front-page story after front-page story, detailing the latest news about the Watergate break-in. Yet, few other media sources covered it. President Nixon and his staff denied all allegations of wrongdoing. A few weeks later, Nixon easily won reelection, despite reports that the Watergate issue was only the tip of the iceberg.

Many thought that now that Nixon was reelected, the Watergate investigation would fade away. But Bernstein and Woodward were just getting started. With the help of Deep Throat, the two continued their investigation, keeping the pressure on the White House to explain the allegations. Other news organizations began covering the story as well.

SENATE INVESTIGATING COMMITTEE

On February 7, 1973, a resolution was passed in the Senate to form the Select Committee on Presidential Campaign Activities. The committee, charged with looking into the possibility of corruption in the 1972 presidential campaign, was led by a Democratic senator from North Carolina, Samuel Ervin.

Senator Ervin, *center*, was also a member on the Constitutional Rights Subcommittee of the Judiciary Committee.

As the committee set to work, President Nixon continued to deny that he had anything to do with the break-in. He also repeatedly claimed that as president, he did not have to comply with the committee's requests for information. When Ervin subpoenaed White House aides to testify before the committee, Nixon refused to allow it. Ervin stated that executive privilege did not extend to criminal acts. On April 30, 1973, three of Nixon's staff resigned in connection to the Watergate scandal.

TELLING THE TRUTH

In May, Archibald Cox, former solicitor general, was made special prosecutor for the Watergate case. Cox called former White House counsel John Dean to testify. Although Nixon still denied any involvement in or knowledge of the break-in, Dean's testimony said otherwise. According to Dean, Nixon had given the go-ahead for White House aides to cover up any involvement with the Watergate break-in. Dean explained to the committee that he and Nixon had talked about the burglary cover-up at least 35 times.

Then, in July 1973, Alexander Butterfield, also a former aide to the president, took the stand. He told the committee that since 1971, the president had a habit of secretly recording conversations using equipment hidden in different rooms throughout the White House. A few days later, Nixon requested that all evidence of the tape recording system be removed from the White House.

The committee, of course, wanted to listen to those tapes. But the president wasn't cooperating—he repeatedly refused to hand them over. Nixon offered to supply the committee with a transcript of the tapes, but Special Prosecutor Cox demanded the tapes themselves.

Nixon finally had enough. On October 20, 1973, in what became known as the Saturday Night Massacre, Nixon ordered Attorney General Elliot Richardson and Deputy Attorney General William Ruckelshaus to fire Cox. Richardson and Ruckelshaus refused to comply and instead resigned. Solicitor General Robert Bork fired Cox instead.

The Watergate scandal was constantly making front-page news.

THE BEGINNING OF THE END

In the wake of the Saturday Night Massacre, Leon Jaworski was assigned to take over Cox's role as special prosecutor. Nixon was then forced by the Supreme Court to finally turn over the transcripts and original tapes to Jaworski. The committee then decided to move forward on impeachment proceedings.

On July 27, 1974, the House Judiciary Committee voted 27 to 11 to impeach Nixon. The president was found guilty of several charges, including obstruction of justice for telling the CIA to hinder an FBI investigation, perjury for lying under oath, obstruction of justice for refusal to turn over evidence,

THE 18.5-MINUTE GAP

Under constant pressure from the press to turn over the tapes of White House conversations to the investigation commission, the Nixon administration finally complied in April 1974. But the tapes were not complete; an 18.5-minute segment of the recording had mysteriously disappeared. This portion of the tape was recorded on June 20, 1972, during a meeting between Nixon and Haldeman. Rose Mary Woods, who had long served as Nixon's personal secretary, told the committee that she had accidentally erased the first five minutes of the conversation while taking a phone call. But when reporters came to the White House to see Woods reenact how that might have happened, it was clear it couldn't have. In the end, the American public never learned what was on that segment of tape nor how it was erased. But it was the press that kept the issue in the news, forcing the administration to provide the requested evidence. In this way, the press worked to keep the executive branch honest.

and wiretapping reporters. On August 8, 1974, before official impeachment proceedings began, President Nixon resigned from office.

FREEDOM OF THE PRESS

This remarkable turn of events was a direct result of the determined investigative reporting of Woodward and Bernstein. This journalist team fully understood the reporter's role as a government watchdog. Freedom of the press, as guaranteed by the First Amendment to the

Constitution, exists to ensure the government does not violate the Constitution.

The American people emerged from the Watergate scandal with a deep distrust of government. But they were not without hope. This dark period in American history inspired an entire generation after watching these events unfold on television. Sara James, one of those journalists, explains the importance of freedom of the press: "We need a 'free press' because we are hardwired to want to know what is going on. Because we need to hold those in power accountable—and because information itself is power. Journalism is about making that power available to everyone, regardless of who you are, or where you live, or what you do, or how much you earn, or who you know. That's why it's an essential liberty."[6]

DISCUSSION STARTERS

- How do you think the Watergate scandal would have played out if journalists hadn't been involved?

- Do you think a president should be exempt from having to cooperate with investigations because he or she has executive privilege? Why or why not?

- Why do you think no other newspapers were covering the Watergate case before the presidential election of 1972?

CHAPTER 2

A ROCKY START FOR FREEDOM

In colonial America, rules related to freedom of the press or free speech mimicked laws and traditions in Britain. There, the monarch oversaw the presses. Before anything could be printed, it had to be approved by the archbishop of Canterbury or the bishop of London. This meant that any information the archbishop did not like or agree with would not be printed. Text that passed the approval process had to be printed at preapproved presses in Oxford, Cambridge, or London, England. Those who were caught violating these printing laws were hauled off to prison and their presses

Johannes Gutenberg invented the first movable type printing press, which dramatically impacted the printing industry, around 1440.

THE STAMP ACT: A FORM OF CENSORSHIP

The Stamp Act of 1765 imposed a tax on all printed material shipped into the American colonies, including books, almanacs, newspapers, blank paper, and playing cards. Britain imposed the tax as a way to recoup expenses that had ratcheted up during the recent Seven Years' War (1756–1763) against France. Because the British defeat of the French had benefitted the American colonies, the British reasoned that the tax was fair. The colonists, however, disagreed, taking to the streets in cities throughout the colonies to stage protests. Journalists in particular spoke out against the tax, claiming the British monarchy was trying to censor the press. Within a few months of November 1, 1765, the date the act was to take effect, Americans had successfully shut down the tax. On March 18, 1766, Parliament voted to repeal the Stamp Act.

were destroyed. Britain also had laws against sedition, or criticizing the government. These laws were enforced even when what was printed or said was the truth.

Printing was introduced in the American colonies in Cambridge, Massachusetts, in 1639. By 1765, publishing had taken off and there were more than 30 presses located throughout the colonies.[1] These presses were subject to many of the same rules applied to presses in Britain, meaning the government censored what the press could print. In the New World, there were sedition laws, too.

JOHN PETER ZENGER

In 1735, John Peter Zenger, a German-born journalist and printer, became a famous example of how the sedition laws were enforced. Zenger was handpicked as the printer for the *New York Weekly Journal* in late 1733. The sole purpose of the journal, which was backed by anonymous members of the Popular Party—James Alexander, William Smith, and Lewis Morris—was to call attention to the corrupt activities and practices of New York Governor William Cosby.

Beginning on November 5, 1733, when the first issue of the *New York Weekly Journal* was released, Alexander, Smith, and Morris published scathing articles that related the intricacies of Governor Cosby's wrongdoings. Cosby put up with the newspaper's reports for a couple of months, but by January 15, 1734, he had enough. He called on Supreme Court Chief Justice DeLancey to charge the journal with seditious libel, or printing damaging stories about public officials, which was against the law in New York. The journal was not found guilty of committing a crime.

In October, Governor Cosby again asked the chief justice to bring charges against the journal, with the same result. Finally, on November 6, Governor Cosby ordered that all copies of the *New York Weekly Journal* be burned in a massive bonfire in front

Zenger's defense in court in 1735

of the city hall. He also put out word that he would pay a sum of 50 pounds to the first person who would give him the names of those responsible for writing the articles printed in the journal. No one stepped forward. So Governor Cosby arrested Zenger, locking him up in the city jail. Zenger was slapped with a lawsuit for publishing critical stories about the governor.

SEE YOU IN COURT

Andrew Hamilton, a well-respected trial lawyer from Philadelphia, Pennsylvania, was chosen to represent Zenger. Deliberations began on August 4, 1735, at the New York city hall. Zenger pleaded not guilty to seditious libel against Governor Cosby. The not guilty plea was surprising to most, as the laws clearly stated that publishing stories that criticized public officials or the government was not permitted. Hamilton's opening argument would go down in history. He eloquently made the case that because what Zenger printed was true, it did not constitute libel. "It is not the cause of one poor printer, but the cause of liberty," Hamilton stated.[2]

The jury deliberated for a mere ten minutes before returning with a verdict of not guilty. Zenger and Hamilton were revered for taking a stand against sedition laws and winning. By overturning this case, the jury laid the foundation for the First Amendment to the Constitution, which would be passed many years later.

PASSING THE FIRST AMENDMENT

The First Amendment was ratified in 1791. It was written by Founding Father and

EARLY BIAS IN THE MEDIA

Bias has always existed in the press to some extent. In early America, it wasn't uncommon for those with money and political opinions to start their own newspaper. Newspapers became the means through which owners could publish their opinions. These early newspapers became the voices of specific political parties, and no one expected the journalists to present objective points of view. The idea of an unbiased media didn't emerge until much later.

future president James Madison with the goal of preventing the government from censoring the press. The First Amendment states:

> *Congress shall make no law respecting an establishment of religion, or prohibiting the free exercise thereof; or abridging the freedom of speech, or of the press; or the right of the people peaceably to assemble, and to petition the Government for a redress of grievances.*[3]

But just what the amendment meant was (and still is) subject to interpretation. Americans were most concerned about government having the ability to censor the press, including prior restraint, a means through which the government prevents a publication from being printed at all. Having lived through the era when journalists who spoke out against the government were arrested and taken to court, Madison approached press freedom differently. By allowing journalists to report about government missteps or corruption, the press took on the unofficial role of government watchdog. If the press was keeping constant tabs on the government, government officials would be more likely to follow the rules set forth in the Constitution.

BRINGING BACK SEDITION LAWS

It wasn't long before freedom of the press was put to the test. By 1798, during John Adams's presidency, partisan

John Adams challenged freedom of the press as second president of the United States.

bickering and fear of the waves of new immigrants entering the country was tearing the United States apart. The United States was also close to going to war with France, which made Americans fearful and uneasy. In advance of the highly contested and partisan election of 1800, Alexander Hamilton and fellow members of the Federalist Party took advantage of this fear, passing a Sedition Act in Congress in 1798. The act reinstated a law that punished people for speaking against the government.

The goal of the sedition law was to prevent newspapers that supported presidential candidate Thomas Jefferson from attacking his opponent, President Adams. During the highly partisan campaign, "Jeffersonian" newspapers cropped up with a clear bias for Jefferson's policies. Jefferson was running as the candidate of the Democratic-Republican Party, which favored more power at the state level than the national level and believed in individual freedoms. His opponent, Adams, was a Federalist, who believed power should be centralized in the hands of the federal government. Jeffersonian newspapers published articles that praised Jefferson while criticizing then-president Adams. The very purpose of these newspapers was to sway public opinion in favor of Jefferson.

The Sedition Act of 1798 was passed specifically to shut down the Jeffersonian newspapers in the months leading up to

PERSPECTIVES
JEFFERSON'S OPINION

Jefferson's opinion of the press was not always favorable. When times got tough during Jefferson's tenure as president and journalists began to cast criticisms in his direction, Jefferson's opinion of the press soured. As president during a politically charged and highly partisan time, Jefferson said, "Nothing can now be believed which is seen in the newspaper. Truth itself becomes suspicious by being put into that polluted vehicle."[4] He even went so far as to use his presidential powers to censor journalists. During his second term, Jefferson took action against the press. In New England newspapers, journalists were publishing harsh words against his policies. Jefferson, in turn, ordered state attorneys general to bring sedition charges against newspaper editors. Jefferson's opinion of the press went back and forth, yet he never wavered from the principle that the press had a role in a democracy and that a free press should be protected. He simply wished journalists would publish objective, true stories without political slants.

John Adams passed the Sedition Act to give more authority to the government in times of war.

the election. Jefferson and James Madison spoke out against the Sedition Act, reminding the American public that the law was a big step back to the shackles of British rule. Together, Jefferson and Madison drafted the Virginia and Kentucky Resolutions, which declared the Sedition Act to be in direct violation of the First and Tenth Amendments.

In the end, Adams lost the election to Jefferson, who became the third president of the United States. When Jefferson took office in 1801, he pardoned those arrested under the Sedition Act. The Supreme Court eventually overturned the act, claiming it violated freedom of the press. "Were it left to me to decide whether we should have a government without newspapers, or newspapers without government," Jefferson stated, "I should not hesitate for a moment to prefer the latter."[5]

DISCUSSION STARTERS

- In colonial America, was there a free press? Why or why not?

- Do you think the government ever has a right to censor newspapers? Why or why not?

- Are newspapers free of bias today? Why or why not?

CHAPTER 3

TIMES OF WAR

The Boston Massacre took place on
March 5, 1770.

Historically, freedom of the press has been restricted during
times of war. The concern was—and still is—that criticism of
the government would present a divided and weakened front
to the enemy.

It's not surprising that Loyalist printers—colonists
who supported the British in the Revolutionary War—were
forbidden to publish pro-British newspaper articles during
the war. The Revolutionary War (1775–1783) happened
before the First Amendment existed. But limitations on press

freedom during wartime continued to color conflicts long after the First Amendment was firmly in effect.

AMERICAN CIVIL WAR (1861–1865)

At the beginning of the American Civil War, US President Abraham Lincoln was quite tolerant of freedom of expression and criticism by the press. Lincoln was often battered by the press, which at different times called him a liar, thief, swindler, tyrant, and monster. The so-called Copperhead press, newspapers run by Southern sympathizers, rose up throughout the Northern states and took aim at the president's policies by publishing vicious attacks. When Lincoln declared martial law in Maryland on April 27, 1861, out of fear that the Confederate troops would overtake Washington, DC, the Copperhead press was not pleased. Then, Supreme Court Chief Justice Roger Taney declared Lincoln's actions unconstitutional. Newspapers within the Copperhead press, including the *New York Tribune*, almost cheered the court action, stating, "the reign of lawless despotism has ended."[1]

Beginning in 1863, some of Lincoln's war generals, including General Ambrose Burnside, who was stationed in Ohio, began to arrest those who spoke out against the president or "declar[ed] sympathies for the enemy."[2] Under General Order 38, Burnside launched a campaign to round

President Lincoln once owned his own newspaper called the Illinois Staats-Anzeiger.

THE *FREE SPEECH AND HEADLIGHT*

In the years between the American Civil War and World War I, small newspapers cropped up around the country to advocate for civil rights. The *Free Speech and Headlight*, an African-American newspaper based in Memphis, Tennessee, was one such publication. Ida B. Wells-Barnett, an African-American woman, became a part owner of the paper in 1892. Using the pen name "Iola," Wells-Barnett spoke out against lynching and voter disenfranchisement. When a friend of hers was lynched for defending a store from a white mob, Wells-Barnett lashed out through articles in her newspaper. She also urged African Americans to leave Memphis in protest. Wells-Barnett left town herself, taking refuge in England, where she spoke about the evils of lynching in America. In 1895, Wells-Barnett published a book titled *The Red Record: Tabulated Statistics and Alleged Causes of Lynching in the United States*. By printing the numbers and details of lynchings, Wells-Barnett hoped to bring much-needed attention to this problem.

up and arrest anti-war protesters. Clement Vallandigham, a former congressman and head of the Peace Democrats, was one of those arrested. Vallandigham had given a speech in Ohio in which he called the president "King Lincoln" and declared that he should be removed from office. In a military court of law, Vallandigham was convicted of a disloyal act and sentenced to spend the rest of the war in prison. But Vallandigham's arrest resulted in violent protests throughout the North, forcing

Lincoln to free Vallandigham from prison and exile him to the South instead.

AS THE WAR RAGED ON

Toward the end of the war, the Lincoln administration began to lose patience with the press. Before 1865, the Union government shuttered more than 300 newspapers in the North that published stories opposing the war.[3] Many newspaper editors were thrown in jail for printing stories that were considered disloyal. In all cases, sentences were handed down not by civil courts, but by military courts, acting under the terms of martial law. In martial law situations, people can be arrested and held without reason if the safety of the nation is thought to be at stake.

Under Order 84, General Burnside shut down the Chicago Times, a paper that slammed Lincoln for his handling of the Vallandigham case. Burnside declared, "Freedom of

FAKE NEWS IN 1864

In May 1864, the Journal of Commerce and the World, both Copperhead press papers based in New York, published a story falsely claiming that President Lincoln was planning to draft another 400,000 men into the Union army. For Lincoln, this was the final straw, and he quickly took action. After having the two papers shut down and the editors arrested, Lincoln took it one step further. He had the military shut down all transmissions from the Independent Telegraph System, which had transmitted the fake news to the wires.

WORLD WAR II (1939–1945)

Unlike the first World War, the American public supported the decision to enter World War II for the most part. The attack on Pearl Harbor was ample justification for going to war against the Japanese, German, and Italian troops. Because of this, there were fewer anti-war protests and fewer instances of anti-war publishing in the press. Those who did criticize President Roosevelt or the war effort were not necessarily arrested and charged. By the 1940s, the government no longer thought it was right to outlaw criticism of the government, even in times of war. But if the criticism was false or contained any information that provided key government secrets to the enemy, the publisher would be brought to court.

discussion and criticism, which is proper . . . in time of peace, becomes rank treason [during wartime] when it tends to weaken . . . confidence."[4] President Lincoln, pressured by public outcry in the North, reopened the newspaper.

WORLD WAR I (1914–1918)

Nearly 50 years later, a now-unified United States was again on the brink of entering a war. This time, however, few Americans were interested in getting involved. President Woodrow Wilson, whose campaign slogan for the 1916 election was "He kept us out of War," had defeated his opponent on that promise.[5] But a year later, the United States entered World War I. The president declared that "the world must be made safe for democracy."[6] The public was not happy.

To win over the American public to the war effort, the Wilson administration launched the Committee on Public Information. The committee published propaganda in the form of leaflets, movies, posters, and commentaries, all designed to stir anti-German sentiments and raise suspicions of anyone who was against the war. Ultimately, the Committee on Public Information's goal was to rally Americans behind the war effort—and stifle anyone who dared to dissent.

One of the propaganda posters used by the Committee on Public Information in World War I

ESPIONAGE AND SEDITION ACTS

On June 15, 1917, the legislature passed the Espionage Act, giving the government the right to control and curtail freedom of the press and speech. And in May 1918,

"CLEAR AND PRESENT DANGER"

One American charged with violating the Espionage Act was Charles Schenck, who was general secretary of the American Socialist Party. His crime? Schenck believed the military draft violated the Thirteenth Amendment, which outlawed slavery. Schenck mailed 15,000 pamphlets to men eligible for the military draft, encouraging them to petition to repeal the draft law.[8] The case went to the Supreme Court, where the justices overwhelmingly ruled in the government's favor. According to Justice Oliver Wendell Holmes, "When a nation is at war, many things that might be said in time of peace are such a hindrance to its effort that their utterance will not be endured so long as men fight and that no Court could regard them as protected by any constitutional right." Schenck's actions, then, posed "a clear and present danger" to the war effort.[9]

the government passed the Sedition Act. These laws made it illegal for citizens to write or publish anything that criticized the president, the Constitution, or anything to do with the war effort. If they did, they were subject to a prison term of 10 to 20 years. At least 2,000 individuals and presses were charged and brought to trial under these laws.[7] In one particular example, the journal *Masses* was strongly opposed to the war. Publishers and editors were arrested and sentenced to prison terms, charged with criticizing the war and the war draft.

Hearing these cases during World War I was the first opportunity the Supreme Court had to interpret the Sedition

Act, which stood in direct conflict with freedom of speech as guaranteed by the First Amendment. But in all cases, the Supreme Court let the convictions stand. The Court asserted that in times of war, freedom of speech and press must be restricted, or people might turn against the war effort and refuse to enter the military. In the end, enforcement of the Sedition and Espionage Acts effectively stopped criticism of the war.

DISCUSSION STARTERS

- Do you agree that press freedom should be restricted in times of war? Why or why not?

- If you were in President Lincoln's shoes, what would you have done about the Copperhead press? Explain your answer.

- Would you consider the actions of the Committee on Public Information during World War I to be honest? Why or why not?

CHAPTER 4

VIETNAM WAR IN THE LIVING ROOM

South Vietnamese soldiers faced tough conditions in the jungle during the Vietnam War, in which an estimated three million people died.

By the time the US government sent troops to Vietnam in the mid-1960s, rules around censorship of the media during times of war had continued to evolve. In World War I and World War II, journalists reporting from the front lines essentially wrote about what the government and military told them to write about. To the contrary, journalists in Vietnam were more of an independent entity. As such, these journalists were sometimes critical of government policies in Vietnam and of the war effort in general.

In Vietnam, more than 2,000 journalists were given free access to the military and had few limitations on where they could go to gather news.[1] Soldiers welcomed reporters and would take them along as they traveled around the country. Reporters built relationships with officers and generals that gave them access to a wealth of information. And the military was not actively trying to restrict or censor journalists. This gave reporters the freedom to provide honest accounts of the war to readers back home. This was something that had never been done before. Journalists were given free rein and could go anywhere and talk to anyone. While this did bring many things to light for Americans back home, it sometimes came at a price. Many journalists died on the battlefield for the sake of a story.

THE WAR IN THE PAPERS

The media made a huge impact on Americans and their perspectives on the Vietnam War. While newspapers were covering the war daily, newsmagazines, such as *Newsweek* and *U.S. News & World Report*, played a slightly different role. They also covered the war constantly, but since the magazines were longer in content, they were able to cover much more. The newsmagazines also brought different perspectives and more details to the forefront.

Two US soldiers read Stars and Stripes, a US military newspaper, in 1969.

While journalists reporting for mainstream media sources had strong opinions on the United States' involvement in the Vietnam War, alternative papers also shouted it out loud and clear. The Black Panther Party (BPP) was a militant African-American organization that supported Ho Chi Minh, a communist leader from Vietnam, in the Vietnam War. The BPP

It became a common pastime for families during the 1960s to gather around the television together and watch the news, especially when stories about the war were on.

criticized the United States for engaging in the Vietnam War. In the *Black Panther Black Community News Service*, an alternative newspaper published by the BPP, Eldridge Cleaver sent a message to black soldiers fighting for the United States: "I know that you . . . have your minds all messed up about Black organizations, or you wouldn't be the flunkies for the white organization—the U.S.A.—for whom you have picked up the gun. The Black Panther Party has picked up the gun too, but not to fight against the heroic Vietnamese people, but rather to wage a war of liberation against the very same pigs whom you are helping to run their vicious game on the entire world, including your own people."[2] Together, mainstream and alternative news outlets presented Americans with a variety of perspectives on the war.

THE WAR ON TELEVISION

The Vietnam War was different from earlier conflicts for another key reason. For the first time, reports from the war were broadcast on television. Whereas only 9 percent of Americans owned a television in 1950, by 1966, 93 percent of Americans owned televisions. A 1964 study indicated that 58 percent of Americans used television as their main source of news.[3]

Each evening American families gathered around televisions to watch half-hour news reports from Vietnam. Although much of the coverage consisted of a reporter sitting at a desk in the newsroom, there was also a fair amount of footage from the front lines. News editors were instructed to strategically review footage for its "queasy quotient," but graphic video of soldiers and civilians suffering did appear on the air.[4]

TOO MUCH FREEDOM?

In past conflicts, government restrictions on press freedoms were enforced to safeguard military secrets and encourage support of the war effort back home. There were few instances in which the reports coming out of Vietnam provided information to the enemy, suggesting that military secrets were protected, despite the more relaxed approach to freedom of the press during the war. But there is plenty of evidence suggesting uncensored, negative media coverage did little to reassure Americans that this was a war they wanted to be supporting. In fact, as the war dragged on, negative media coverage, especially television footage showing dead American soldiers, turned more and more Americans against the war.

In addition to footage of soldiers in battle and daily reports of deaths and casualties from the newsroom, journalists used television to convey other aspects of the war. In one *CBS Evening News* report, for example, a young American woman who had just lost her husband in the war read the last letter she received from him on camera. As she read, she held the couple's baby in her arms. In another instance, CBS reporter Morley Safer went along with an American platoon on a seek-and-destroy mission in which the soldiers had been ordered to burn a Vietnamese village to the ground. As the homes burned, the cameraman panned to the emotional Vietnamese families who were left homeless. With these images, the press influenced public opinion, turning more Americans against the war.

THE 5 O'CLOCK FOLLIES

Throughout the Vietnam War, the military gave daily briefings to journalists at the Rex Hotel in Saigon. A spokesman for the Pentagon stood in front of a microphone and recited the number of enemy soldiers killed and listed other statistics that supported the notion that the United States and Southern Vietnamese forces were winning the war. The journalists in attendance began to refer to the briefings as "the 5 o'clock follies," as many believed the reports didn't provide a complete picture of what was really going on. Since the Vietnam War, the term has been used to describe the difficult process of trying to put the best spin on a bad situation: a nation at war. During World Wars I and II, briefings from the military provided all the information journalists had to report on the war, and during the Vietnam War, there were many journalists who relied on these daily briefings. But there were several others who struck out on their own to report the war as they saw it.

PRESS POOLS

As a result of the perceived damage inflicted on the war effort by the journalists in Vietnam, the Bush administration instated new rules for the press reporting on the 1990 war in Iraq. First, reporters were assigned to press "pools" of approximately 18 reporters each.[5] Press pools were not allowed into the field without an escort, nor could they interview military personnel without an escort present. Once a story was written, the text was reviewed by a "military security review system," a process by which sensitive or damaging information was deleted or changed.[6] Reporters could appeal the changes. Reporters who broke the press pool rules were subject to arrest, detention, and revocation of press passes/credentials, and they could be sent home. Journalists protested these limitations, stating that they were not allowed to visit scenes where American soldiers had been killed. Reporters also objected to the military escorts who tried to influence military personnel to answer press questions in a certain way or sometimes answered for them. All of these instances, journalists claimed, violated freedom of the press.

However, many thought the media had crossed the line when NBC televised the execution of a suspected informant on the evening news. The video rolls as General Loan, a known ally of the Americans, places a gun to the man's temple and pulls the trigger. Blood can be seen flowing from the man's head as he falls dead in the street. NBC journalist John Chancellor vividly remembers the first time he saw the footage and how it was perceived by audiences back home. "The execution was added to people's feeling that this is just horrible, this is just terrible. Why are we involved in a thing like this? People were just sickened by it. And I think that added to the feeling that the war was the wrong war in the wrong place."[7]

TURNING POINT

A major shift in media coverage of the war came after the Tet Offensive, which began on January 31, 1968. In the largest military assault of the war, North Vietnam and the Vietcong, the North's Communist allies in South Vietnam, launched a surprise attack on the cities of Saigon and Hue and many other areas of the South. Although the Communists technically lost the battle, suffering 40,000 casualties, media reports suggested otherwise. On evening news reports, American audiences watched footage showing the attack and seizure of the US embassy in Saigon. Again, they saw dead American soldiers on television.

But it was the words of trusted journalist Walter Cronkite that would fuel anti-war protests and turn even more Americans against the war in Vietnam. On February 27, 1968, Cronkite said of the Tet Offensive, "The Vietcong did not win by a knockout, but neither did we. . . . We are mired in stalemate."[8]

This was the beginning of the end of civilian support for the war, and President Lyndon B. Johnson knew it. "If I've

Walter Cronkite was an anchor on the *CBS Evening News* for nearly 20 years.

lost Cronkite, I've lost Middle America," Johnson said.[9] Shortly thereafter, Johnson announced he would not be seeking another term as president.

In the end, the military would blame the press for "losing Vietnam."[10] Had Americans not been subjected to the daily images of death and destruction on television, the military claimed, they would not have turned against the war. The Pentagon vowed to restrict freedom of the press in the future.

DISCUSSION STARTERS

- Why was the Vietnam War called the living room war? Explain why you think this impacted the American public's opinions of the war.

- Do you think it was right or wrong for NBC News to play a video of an execution on the air? Explain your answer.

- If the *Black Panther Black Community News Service* had been published during World War I, the Panthers would have been arrested and the paper shut down. Do you think the US government should have taken actions against them during the Vietnam War? Why or why not?

- Why do you think freedom of the press was allowed during the Vietnam War? What had changed?

CHAPTER 5

CENSORSHIP AND PRIOR RESTRAINT

The US Supreme Court has the final say in issues that affect the government and US citizens.

When crafting the First Amendment, James Madison and the Founding Fathers were particularly concerned about censorship and prior restraint. Censorship is the process by which the government reviews and identifies information from news articles, books, or any other form of media that should not be shared with the public. Prior restraint occurs when the government prevents presses from publishing information that the government deems sensitive. Both practices, which prevailed under British rule, were also used in colonial and early America.

The Founding Fathers, however, were against censorship and prior restraint. They considered a free press to be vital to a healthy democracy. Only with freedom of the press guaranteed by the First Amendment would journalists be able to identify and call out instances in which the government was violating or threatening to violate the Constitution. In this role, the press almost acts as a fourth branch of government, keeping the executive, legislative, and judicial branches in check.

THE SUPREME COURT AND PRIOR RESTRAINT

According to the Supreme Court, prior restraints are "the most serious and least tolerable infringement on First Amendment rights."[1] Because of this, when cases of prior restraint come before the Supreme Court, the justices almost always find the restraint to be in violation of the Constitution.

But there are a few instances when prior restraint is considered justified. Offensive sexual material, for example, is not protected by the First Amendment, as courts have deemed this material has no value to society. Anything that threatens national security, as determined by the Justice Department and the Supreme Court, is also not protected by the First Amendment. And, in times of war, the press cannot publish details about troop locations, plans to attack, or anything else that threatens the war effort.

MINNESOTA GAG LAW

One key Supreme Court case laid the foundation for future rulings. *Near v. Minnesota*, decided in 1931, challenged a controversial law called the Minnesota Gag Law. The law stated that

Supreme Court Chief Justice Charles E. Hughes passed down the decision in *Near v. Minnesota*.

anyone who publishes and distributes an "obscene, lewd and lascivious" or a "malicious, scandalous and defamatory" newspaper or other printed material is considered a "nuisance," and will be ordered to stop publication.[2] Those who disobeyed were required to pay a fine or serve prison time.

The case of *Near v. Minnesota* was brought against a weekly newspaper published in Minneapolis, the *Saturday Press*. The Hennepin County attorney who brought the suit claimed that the paper published only scandalous and defamatory articles. More specifically, the county attorney had an issue with an article claiming that a Jewish gangster was running gambling, bootlegging, and racketeering operations in Minneapolis and that local law enforcement was not trying hard enough to bring the gangster to justice.

At the state level, the *Saturday Press* was found to be a nuisance under the Minnesota Gag Law. The Supreme Court, however, decided otherwise. In a 5–4 ruling, the court declared this to be an example of prior restraint, or "effective censorship," and in violation of the First Amendment.[3]

In the 1930s, newspapers were often sold to people on the street.

GROSJEAN V. AMERICAN PRESS CO.

A second case, heard by the Supreme Court in 1936, reinforced the court's stand on another aspect of prior restraint. In *Grosjean v. American Press Co.*, nine newspaper publishers together filed a suit to fight a law requiring that any business involved in making or charging for advertisements that had a circulation of 20,000 copies per week pay a license tax. Those businesses (newspaper or other print media) that did not pay the tax faced a fine or prison term or both.

The court ruled that the law imposed a double restraint on newspapers. One form of restraint was setting a limit on the amount the paper could earn through advertising. The second restraint limited circulation of the newspaper, which directly infringed on freedom of the press.

LOVELL V. GRIFFIN

A third case taken to the Supreme Court brought up a new issue with government censorship: the printing of religious materials. In 1938, the city of Griffin, Georgia, had an ordinance that required everyone to get permission from the city government before passing out any printed material. One day Alma Lovell, a Jehovah's Witness, began passing out religious pamphlets to people on the street. However, Lovell was immediately arrested. The city cited that she did not get permission to pass out these materials.

The case then went all the way up to the Supreme Court, which decided that Lovell did in fact have a right to pass out any religious printed materials she wanted. The Court then stated that, "The press, in its historic connotation, comprehends every sort of publication which affords a vehicle of information and opinion."[4] So then, it was a form of prior restraint by the city to require permission to distribute any printed materials.

PENTAGON PAPERS

One of the primary examples of the government issuing prior restraint to protect national security occurred during the

The *New York Times* printed many articles on the Pentagon Papers.

Vietnam War. In 1967, as the war was becoming increasingly controversial, US secretary of defense Robert McNamara asked the Defense Department to provide a full report of the US government's involvement in Vietnam. The report, which would become known as the Pentagon Papers, included classified information gathered from the CIA, the State Department, and the Defense Department. The resulting document, which was completed in 1969, included 7,000 pages.

The report revealed that the United States had been involved in Vietnam since President Harry Truman decided to provide military aid to France in its fight against the Communist Viet Minh between 1946 and 1954. Presidents Dwight D. Eisenhower, John F. Kennedy, and Johnson had all lied to the American public about the level of US involvement in Vietnam. But were they acting in the interest of national security, or did the American public have a right to know?

Military analyst Daniel Ellsberg, a former US Marines officer, worked at the Defense Department at the time.

FREEDOM OF INFORMATION ACT

The Freedom of Information Act, passed into law on July 4, 1966, states that any person has the right to request access to federal records or information kept on file with the US government. Not all information can be accessed, however. Classified information that would pose a risk to national security, for example, is not available. The need for such a law arose during the Cold War era of the 1950s, when American citizens were becoming increasingly suspicious of the information the government was gathering about them. This law also made it possible for investigative journalists to obtain documents and information needed to accurately report the news.

As he read the report, he decided the public should know the truth about Vietnam. Ellsberg secretly photocopied the pages over nearly two years. Throughout that time, he offered the pages to different members of Congress, all of whom refused to take action on the information. Then in 1971, Ellsberg met with Neil Sheehan, a *New York Times* reporter. Three months later, the *Times* began to publish a series of articles based on the Pentagon Papers.

GOING TO COURT

When the *New York Times* published a third Pentagon Papers article, the Nixon administration invoked prior restraint, issuing a restraining order on the *Times*. The Justice Department claimed that the release of the information threatened national security. But other newspapers started publishing excerpts of the Pentagon Papers too, including the *Washington Post*. When the government continued to try to block the newspapers from reporting the classified government documents, the *Times* and the *Post* took the issue all the way to the Supreme Court.

On June 30, 1971, in a 6–3 ruling, the Supreme Court decided in favor of the *New York Times* and *Washington Post*, granting the *Times* permission to print the Pentagon Papers. The court argued that if administrations could withhold information from the American public, government censorship

DANIEL ELLSBERG

Daniel Ellsberg, a former officer in the US Marines and strategic military analyst for the RAND Corporation, was a key figure in the Pentagon Papers case. At the beginning of the war in Vietnam, Ellsberg firmly believed the war was necessary and that the United States had every reason to be involved. Ellsberg had grown up during the Cold War and supported American efforts to triumph over Communism. But the more Ellsberg learned about Vietnam, the more those beliefs began to change. A pivotal moment came in 1965, when Ellsberg became special liaison to Major General Edward G. Lansdale in Vietnam. With this insider look at US policy and decision-making at the ground level, Ellsberg began to believe that the war could not be won if the United States continued on its current course. After the Tet Offensive and the assassinations of Martin Luther King Jr. and Robert Kennedy in 1968, Ellsberg made up his mind to do what he could to end the Vietnam War. In the name of press freedom, he leaked information about US involvement in the war to the *New York Times*. Ellsberg thought Americans deserved to know the truth.

would only escalate in the future. In this landmark victory for freedom of the press, the Supreme Court once again found the government's prior restraint order to be in violation of the Constitution.

RIGHT TO A FAIR TRIAL

Another instance in which prior restraint commonly surfaces is during court cases, when judges are concerned that press coverage of a trial will infringe on the defendant's Sixth Amendment rights, which guarantee the right to a fair trial. The concern is that if information about the trial is reported by the press and jurors follow the news and form an opinion on the events, they may develop a bias about the case.

REPORTER'S PRIVILEGE

In 1972, the Supreme Court handed down a ruling on four combined cases, called *Branzburg v. Hayes*, that involved reporter's privilege. Journalists argued that they should not have to testify in grand jury cases, or cases that investigate potential criminal conduct, as this infringes on press freedom. Journalists stuck to this belief, even if their sources had been involved in criminal activity. The court ruled against the journalists, however. The court decided that anyone who has information about a grand jury trial must share it, just like every other citizen. Journalists still fear that if they cannot keep sources secret, no one will provide information. If they are unable to gather information, freedom of the press is ultimately compromised.

In the 1976 case *Nebraska Press Association v. Stuart*, the lower court attempted to protect the rights of the defendant by issuing a gag order, which prevents the press from covering a trial. In this case the defendant, who was on trial for murder, had confessed to the crime to police. The judge issued a restraint to the press to prevent it from televising or printing the confession, as he believed it would ruin any chances for a fair trial. But the Supreme Court unanimously overruled the gag order, arguing that an entire small town, the town of Sutherland, Nebraska, could not be prevented from talking about a murder that so deeply affected their lives.

DISCUSSION STARTERS

- Did Daniel Ellsberg do the right thing when he handed parts of the Pentagon Papers over to the *New York Times*? Why or why not?

- Should journalists be forced to testify in grand jury cases? Explain your answer.

- Why do you think the Supreme Court considers prior restraints "the most serious and least tolerable infringement on First Amendment rights"?

> *"The growing movement of peaceful mass demonstrations by Negroes is something new in the South, something understandable.... Let Congress heed their rising voices, for they will be heard."*
>
> —New York Times editorial
> Saturday, March 19, 1960

Heed Their Rising Voices

As the whole world knows by now, thousands of Southern Negro students are engaged in widespread non-violent demonstrations in positive affirmation of the right to live in human dignity as guaranteed by the U. S. Constitution and the Bill of Rights. In their efforts to uphold these guarantees, they are being met by an unprecedented wave of terror by those who would deny and negate that document which the whole world looks upon as setting the pattern for modern freedom....

In Orangeburg, South Carolina, when 400 students peacefully sought to buy doughnuts and coffee at lunch counters in the business district, they were forcibly ejected, tear-gassed, soaked to the skin in freezing weather with fire hoses, arrested en masse and herded into an open barbed-wire stockade to stand for hours in the bitter cold.

In Montgomery, Alabama, after students sang "My Country, 'Tis of Thee" on the State Capitol steps, their leaders were expelled from school, and truckloads of police armed with shotguns and tear-gas ringed the Alabama State College Campus. When the entire student body protested to state authorities by refusing to re-register, their dining hall was padlocked in an attempt to starve them into submission.

In Tallahassee, Atlanta, Nashville, Savannah, Greensboro, Memphis, Richmond, Charlotte, and a host of other cities in the South, young American teenagers, in face of the entire weight of official state apparatus and police power, have boldly stepped forth as protagonists of democracy. Their courage and amazing restraint have inspired millions and given a new dignity to the cause of freedom.

Small wonder that the Southern violators of the Constitution fear this new, non-violent brand of freedom fighter ... even as they fear the upswelling right-to-vote movement. Small wonder that they are determined to destroy the one man who, more than any other, symbolizes the new spirit now sweeping the South—the Rev. Dr. Martin Luther King, Jr., world-famous leader of the Montgomery Bus Protest. For it is his doctrine of non-violence which has inspired and guided the students in their widening wave of sit-ins; and it is this same Dr. King who founded and is president of the Southern Christian Leadership Conference—the organization which is spearheading the surging right-to-vote movement. Under Dr. King's direction the Leadership Conference conducts Student Workshops and Seminars in the philosophy and technique of non-violent resistance.

Again and again the Southern violators have answered Dr. King's peaceful protests with intimidation and violence. They have bombed his home almost killing his wife and child. They have assaulted his person. They have arrested him seven times—for "speeding," "loitering" and similar "offenses." And now they have charged him with "perjury"—a *felony* under which they could imprison him for *ten years*. Obviously, their real purpose is to remove him physically as the leader to whom the students and millions of others—look for guidance and support, and thereby to intimidate *all* leaders who may rise in the South. Their strategy is to behead this affirmative movement and thus to demoralize Negro Americans and weaken their will to struggle. The defense of Martin Luther King, spiritual leader of the student sit-in movement clearly, therefore, is an integral part of the total struggle for freedom in the South.

Decent-minded Americans cannot help but applaud the creative daring of the students and the quiet heroism of Dr. King. But this is one of those moments in the stormy history of Freedom when men and women of good will must do more than applaud the rising-to-glory of others. The America whose good name hangs in the balance before a watchful world, the America whose heritage of Liberty these Southern Upholders of the Constitution are defending, is *our* America as well as theirs ...

We must heed their rising voices—yes—but we must add our own.

We must extend ourselves above and beyond moral support and render the material help so urgently needed by those who are taking the risks, facing jail, and even death in a glorious re-affirmation of our Constitution and its Bill of Rights.

We urge you to join hands with our fellow Americans in the South by supporting, with your dollars, this Combined Appeal for all three needs—the defense of Martin Luther King—the support of the embattled students—and the struggle for the right-to-vote.

Your Help Is Urgently Needed ... NOW!!

Stella Adler
Raymond Pace Alexander
Shelly Appleton
Harry Van Andale
Harry Belafonte
Julie Belafonte
Dr. Algernon Black
Marc Blitzstein
William Bowe
William Branch
Marlon Brando
Mrs. Ralph Bunche
Diahann Carroll
Dr. Alan Knight Chalmers

Joseph Cohen
Richard Coe
Nat King Cole
Cheryl Crawford
Dorothy Dandridge
Ossie Davis
Sammy Davis, Jr.
Ruby Dee
Harry Dufty
Scotty Eckford
Dr. Philip Elliott
Dr. Harry Emerson Fosdick

Anthony Franciosa
Mathew Guinan
Lorraine Hansbury
Rev. Donald Harrington
Nat Hentoff
James Hicks
Mary Hinkson
Van Heflin
Langston Hughes
Morris Iushewitz
Mahalia Jackson
Paul Jennings
Mordecai Johnson
John Killens

Eartha Kitt
Rabbi Edward Klein
Hope Lange
John Lewis
Viveca Lindfors
David Livingston
William Michoelson
Carl Murphy
Don Murray
John Murray
A. J. Muste
Frederick O'Neal
Peter Ottley
L. Joseph Overton

Albert P. Palmer
Clarence Pickett
Shad Polier
Sidney Poitier
Michael Potoker
A. Philip Randolph
John Raitt
Elmer Rice
Cleveland Robinson
Jackie Robinson
Mrs. Eleanor Roosevelt
Bayard Rustin
Robert Ryan
Maureen Stapleton

Frank Silvera
Louis Simon
Hope Stevens
David Sullivan
Julius Sum
George Tabori
Rev. Gardner C. Taylor
Norman Thomas
Kenneth Tynan
Charles White
Shelley Winters
Max Youngstein

We in the south who are struggling daily for dignity and freedom warmly endorse this appeal

Rev. Ralph D. Abernathy
(Montgomery, Ala.)

Rev. Fred L. Shuttlesworth
(Birmingham, Ala.)

Rev. Kelley Miller Smith
(Nashville, Tenn.)

Rev. W. A. Dennis
(Chattanooga, Tenn.)

Rev. C. K. Steele
(Tallahassee, Fla.)

Rev. Matthew D. McCollom
(Orangeburg, S. C.)

Rev. William Holmes Borders
(Atlanta, Ga.)

Rev. Douglas Moore
(Durham, N. C.)

Rev. Wyatt Tee Walker
(Petersburg, Va.)

Rev. Walter L. Hamilton
(Norfolk, Va.)

I. S. Levy
(Columbia, S. C.)

Rev. Martin Luther King, Sr.
(Atlanta, Ga.)

Rev. Henry C. Bunton
(Memphis, Tenn.)

Rev. S. S. Seay, Sr.
(Montgomery, Ala.)

Rev. Samuel W. Williams
(Atlanta, Ga.)

Rev. A. L. Davis
(New Orleans, La.)

Mrs. Katie E. Whickham
(New Orleans, La.)

Rev. W. H. Hall
(Hattiesburg, Miss.)

Rev. J. E. Lowery
(Mobile, Ala.)

Rev. T. J. Jemison
(Baton Rouge, La.)

Please mail this coupon TOI

Committee To Defend Martin Luther K
and
The Struggle For Freedom In The So

312 West 125th Street, New York 27, N
UNiversity 6-1700

I am enclosing my contribution of $........
for the work of the Committee.

Name ....
(PLEASE PRINT)

Address ....

City .... Zone .... State ....

☐ I want to help   ☐ Please send further information

COMMITTEE TO DEFEND MARTIN LUTHER KING AND THE STRUGGLE FOR FREEDOM IN THE SOUTH
312 West 125th Street, New York 27, N. Y. UNiversity 6-1700

Chairmen: A. Philip Randolph, Dr. Gardner C. Taylor; *Chairmen of Cultural Division: Harry Belafonte*

CHAPTER 6

LIBEL

Libel, the publication of false or defamatory statements about an individual that harms the person's reputation, was at the heart of the landmark Supreme Court case *New York Times Co. v. Sullivan* in 1964. The case focused on an advertisement printed in the Tuesday, March 29, 1960, edition of the *New York Times*.

The ad's headline read, "Heed Their Rising Voices."[1] It encouraged readers to provide financial support to the civil rights demonstrators in the South. The demonstrators were peacefully working toward equal treatment for all Americans,

An ad that ran in the *New York Times* in 1960 led to what is considered one of the most significant cases for freedom of the press.

no matter the color of their skin. These demonstrators, the ad claimed, had been mistreated by local law enforcement in Orangeburg, South Carolina, and Montgomery, Alabama. The ad included the names of many celebrities who endorsed the movement, such as Martin Luther King Jr., Nat King Cole, Harry Belafonte, Shelley Winters, Jackie Robinson, and Eleanor Roosevelt. It was a powerful plea on behalf of the civil rights movement.

But not everyone agreed with the claims made in the ad. Montgomery commissioner L. B. Sullivan strongly objected to some of the statements, claiming they were downright false. Sullivan, who led the Montgomery police department, stepped forward to correct false claims that students

LIBEL'S HISTORY

The first libel laws can be traced back to a legal argument put forth by Alexander Hamilton. Back in 1804, a time when defaming a public official was considered a crime, Hamilton stepped up to defend Harry Croswell. Croswell was the editor of a newspaper called *Wasp*, which had published a few unflattering comments about President Jefferson.

As it turned out, Croswell's seemingly spiteful words about Jefferson were true. Hamilton argued that "the liberty of publishing truth, with good motives and for justifiable ends, even though it reflects on government, magistrates, or private persons," should be a freedom all Americans can enjoy.[2] Although Hamilton lost the case, a year later legislators from New York passed a law that a person cannot sue for libel if published statements are, in fact, true.

were not allowed to enter a dining hall during a protest and that armed police surrounded the campus. Both statements were not true. Beyond the fact that the ad included inaccuracies, Sullivan and many other white officials in the South were deeply offended by the ad. Sullivan claimed the ad harmed his reputation by directly attacking the way in which local law enforcement handled the civil rights protests, accusing the police of brutality. When Sullivan decided to sue the *New York Times* for libel, others got in line behind him. Sullivan won the case in an Alabama court, and the *New York Times* was required to pay him $500,000 in damages.[3] But the *Times* appealed the case to the Supreme Court.

Sullivan, *second from left*, smiled with his attorneys after he was awarded $500,000 in damages.

65

A VICTORY FOR FREE PRESS

The case became a monumental victory for freedom of the press. The *New York Times* successfully argued that if the press had to check the accuracy of every statement, freedom of the press would be "severely limited." Under the First Amendment, newspapers are protected from lawsuits in instances when they print inaccurate information, as long as the mistakes are unintentional and not done with malice. This doesn't give journalists a license to be careless in their reporting. When errors are made, journalists are expected to publish retractions. This is a notice that calls attention to the error and provides the correct information. In examining libel cases, courts consider the following points: defamatory nature of statements, how they were published, whether the claims are true or false, whether they concern an individual, the harm caused, and the degree of fault.

Libel, the court argued, covers celebrities and public officials whose reputations are at stake. However, the burden of proof is on the celebrity or official. This means the person claiming to be a victim of libel must prove that the press acted with malice or intent to harm when it published false or damaging information about him or her, which is very difficult to prove. Ordinary citizens can also sue for libel even if the press unknowingly printed incorrect information about them.

In the decision, the Supreme Court stressed that the freedom to openly discuss and criticize the actions and policies of public officials is more important than the inadvertent factual errors that sometimes occur in print. Justice William Brennan Jr. wrote, "Public discussion is a political duty, and . . . this should be a fundamental principle of the American government."[4]

According to Kenneth A. Paulson, president and CEO of the First Amendment Center at the Newseum in Washington, DC, the *Sullivan* decision carried a great weight among journalists. The ruling "freed up news organizations to

TRUTH VS. FICTION

The *New York Times Co. v. Sullivan* case is interesting because the supposed instances of libel occurred in a paid advertisement rather than a news article that was written by a *New York Times* journalist. What is the difference? Paid advertising content has a different purpose than newspaper articles. Companies or organizations that pay to place ads in a newspaper have an agenda— their goal is to convince the reader to buy a product, take a specific action, or, as in the case of the civil rights ad, give money to a cause. News articles, on the other hand, have a specific purpose to inform the reader of news and events in an objective manner. Articles printed in the newspaper are presumed to be based on fact, unless those articles are labeled "editorial" or "opinion," meaning the article includes that author's own opinion on the subject.

pursue the stories that needed pursuing. It allows you to write the stories about the local [businesspeople] who don't want you questioning their ethics and stories about the mayor who doesn't want you to ask about a relative who is on the payroll."[5]

KAELIN V. GLOBE COMMUNICATIONS CORPORATION

While it is difficult to prove libel, there have been cases where a court has ruled in favor of the person citing libel. In 1995, the nation was gripped with the story of professional football player O. J. Simpson and the murder of his wife Nicole Brown Simpson. O. J. was soon arrested for her murder but, after a long and infamous trial, he was acquitted of all charges. This caused many people to look frantically for someone else who could have possibly been the killer.

Brian "Kato" Kaelin, a friend of the Simpsons, was then brought under the microscope. While the police eventually ruled him out as a suspect, the *National Examiner* published a front-page news story a week after Simpson's acquittal with the headline, "Cops Think Kato Did It."[6] The headline and entire article led people to believe that Kaelin was still a suspect in the police's eyes and that he committed perjury by lying on the stand. Kaelin then sued the newspaper's publisher, Globe Communications Corporation, for libel. The court ruled that

Kato Kaelin proved that just a headline can cause libel.

Many celebrities and politicians have filed libel lawsuits, including First Lady Melania Trump against the newspaper the *Daily Mail* in 2017.

because the police (and also the newspaper) did not actually think that Kaelin committed the murders, the newspaper knowingly published a false story. The court also concluded, "The article, including the headline and caption and taking into account the circumstances of its publication, is reasonably susceptible of a defamatory meaning on its face and therefore is libelous."[7]

LIBEL LAWS THREATENED

In 2016 and 2017, the nation's libel laws came under fire from newly elected President Donald Trump, who pledged to "open up our libel laws."[8] Trump wanted to make it easier for people to file lawsuits when the press makes unflattering comments about them.

TABLOID LAWSUITS

The headlines that blare from the front covers of tabloid newspapers in supermarket checkout lines can't possibly be true. So how do the publishers get away with it? The answer lies in the strength of libel laws, which put the burden of proof firmly into the hands of the celebrity victims. To win court cases against lawyers representing the interests of tabloids such as the *National Enquirer* or the *Star*, lawyers representing celebrities must prove that the tabloid knowingly published false information about their client with the intent to defame them. This is difficult to do. Not only will the suit likely cost the celebrity hundreds of thousands of dollars, but his or her life will also be open to intense scrutiny in the process. Often, it's simply not worth the hassle.

This may be easier said than done, however. Libel laws are established by each state and protected by the First Amendment. These laws protect journalists from lawsuits. Any changes to the current laws would need to happen in the legislature or in the courts, not in the executive branch. One look at the voting record of Supreme Court Justice Judge Neil M. Gorsuch makes the situation even more interesting.

Neil M. Gorsuch has served as a judge in many libel cases in the past.

The judge, who was nominated by Trump himself in January 2017, has a strong record of voting to protect First Amendment rights, including libel. The Trump administration may have an uphill climb when it comes to this battle.

The effect of the *Sullivan* ruling on the media was significant. The *Sullivan* case not only expanded press freedom, but it also served to reaffirm the media's role as a government watchdog. In the decades following the ruling, investigative journalism experienced a boom, as more and more young people entered the field. Having grown up during the time of the Vietnam War and the Watergate scandal, this generation of journalists understood the media's role in keeping the government honest and in check. But in the wake of the 9/11 attacks on the World Trade Center in 2001, times have changed. The American mind-set has shifted from protecting press freedom to preventing information leaks in the name of enforcing national security.

DISCUSSION STARTERS

- Do you think it's fair that newspapers can't be sued for inaccuracies in their stories? Why or why not?

- Why do you think celebrities and public officials are treated differently in libel cases than ordinary citizens?

- The Trump administration has promised to hold the media accountable by tightening libel laws. If it is able to do so, how do you think freedom of the press would be affected?

CHAPTER 7

FREEDOM OF THE PRESS AND THE INTERNET

Members of *Time* magazine's online edition, which began after the Internet came into wider use in 1994

The rise of the Internet in the 1990s ushered in many new issues pertaining to freedom of the press. As more and more homes gained access to Internet services, the World Wide Web fundamentally changed the way Americans got their news.

Easy access to online sources caused shake-ups within the newspaper industry, resulting in a decline in the circulation of traditional newspapers in the past several years. In 2015 alone, circulation fell by 7 percent.[1] More people are getting their news through digital online news sources, leading to layoffs in newsrooms nationwide. Even news programs on television are in decline. More and more people are leaning toward faster, more immediate news. In fact, in 2017, 67 percent of American adults looked to social media to learn what was happening around the world. Facebook is the leading provider of online news.[2]

The Internet has also affected the quality of news. Although major newspapers have transitioned to digital formats, they share web space with countless other news sources, including sites such as Wikipedia and even personal websites. However, the content of these sites isn't always accurate or reliable.

The Internet, then, becomes hard to police. It is a place where free speech and freedom of the press blur together. If the "press" is determined by the Supreme Court as "every publication

CONGLOMERATE NEWS

As budgets tighten at newsrooms, conglomerate buyouts have become increasingly common. This means several newspapers, either in a specific area of the country or nationwide, may be owned by the same parent company—and may be under the control of one executive or owner who oversees operations. Although newspapers within the group vary in coverage to include stories that apply to their region, the overarching philosophy or approach to the news remains the same between papers within the group. This limits the exchange of diverse viewpoints, which ultimately hinders freedom of the press.

which affords a vehicle of information and opinion," the Internet then surely is included in that spectrum.[3] But how can it be monitored or held accountable for the information that is posted? Is everything then fair game when it comes to using the web? The answer is up for debate.

NET NEUTRALITY

Allowing access, choice, and transparency of Internet offerings is essential to press freedom and freedom of speech. As the Internet evolves, however, it is shifting from

Net neutrality stops large Internet service providers, such as Verizon, Comcast, and AT&T, from determining which sites users can and can't access.

the uncensored platform for free speech it was in the early days of the mid-1990s to one that's controlled and monitored by corporations.

In 2015, the administration of President Barack Obama passed rules that strictly regulated cable and telecom companies that provide Internet services to customers. These regulations enforced net neutrality, the concept of keeping the Internet open and free and offering equal access to all sites.

The election of President Donald Trump in November 2016 brought changes to leadership at the Federal Communications Commission (FCC), the government entity that regulates the broadcast industries. In May 2017, new FCC chief Ajit Pai proposed rolling back the Obama-era regulations. Without the regulations in place, Internet providers

NEUTRALITY LOOPHOLES

It may be that a rollback of net neutrality rules won't significantly change access after all. In a May 2017 court case involving US Telecom Association, the FCC, and the Independent Telephone & Telecommunications Alliance, Washington, DC, circuit court judges ruled that the net neutrality rules put in place by the Obama administration still allow Internet providers to filter content and even direct content into fast and slow lanes, as long as they openly state that they are doing so. Essentially, the rules have been more flexible than both proponents and opponents have realized. In the end, it's a net loss for freedom of the press.

would have the authority to block access to specific websites or apps and throttle—or slow down—loading speeds without government oversight.

Under the proposed rollback, Internet providers would have the right to block and filter—pick and choose—which websites they allow access to based on regulatory controls or their own business objectives. Blocking access limits freedom of the press. Consider the case of AT&T, an Internet provider and supporter of conservative organizations such as the American Legislative Exchange Council. If net neutrality regulations are rolled back, the company could effectively deny web access to websites that publish policies and opinions it doesn't agree with. Supporters of the rollback argue that by allowing websites to be blocked, minors can be protected from objectionable content and illegal content can be more effectively regulated. Those in favor of this rollback also feel the government should have more control over Americans' Internet usage.

WIKILEAKS

The age of the Internet has also provided a platform through which journalists—either professional or not—may quickly and effectively disseminate information to a wide audience. The widely accessible environment of the Internet gave rise to a media association called WikiLeaks. The company, founded by

"COULD BECOME AS IM

WikiLeaks is still a live and active site, continuing to publish controversial information.

Julian Assange in 2006, defines its mission as electronically distributing original documents submitted by anonymous sources. There is one caveat: the material must have "political, ethical, diplomatic, or historical significance."[4]

In February 2010, US Army intelligence analyst Private Bradley Manning (now Chelsea Manning) released hundreds of thousands of classified documents from the CIA and

State Department to WikiLeaks. Assange began to publish

the content online through WikiLeaks, first releasing a video

that showed US soldiers shooting 18 Iraqi civilians from

a helicopter.

When Manning confessed to leaking classified information

online to computer hacker Adrian Lamo, Lamo contacted the

Defense Department. Manning was arrested in May 2010 and

charged with espionage, theft, and computer fraud. Manning denied any intention of causing harm to the United States but wanted to instead begin a conversation and debate about the released information. Manning was sentenced to 35 years in prison—an extreme sentence for a whistle-blower. Manning was released after serving a seven-year sentence that included solitary confinement.[5]

There have been murmurs of pressing charges against Assange for releasing classified information. But this has not been done before. "Never in the history of this country has a publisher

EDWARD SNOWDEN

Another high-profile whistle-blowing case involved Edward Snowden, a systems analyst who was employed by a government contractor. After learning that the US National Security Agency (NSA) had been gathering the phone records of tens of millions of Americans, Snowden decided to leak the information to the *Guardian* newspaper in June 2013. The resulting article that appeared in the *Guardian* included a court order from the NSA requesting that telecommunications company Verizon send telephone records to the agency each day. Later, articles in the *Washington Post* and the *Guardian* revealed that the NSA had tapped into an entire network of Internet companies, including Facebook, Google, and Microsoft, to trace conversations between customers. For leaking the information, Snowden was charged with "theft of government property, unauthorized communication of national defense information, and willful communication of classified communications intelligence."[6] Snowden was granted safety in Russia.

been prosecuted for presenting truthful information to the public," explained Ben Wizner of the American Civil Liberties Union. "Any prosecution of WikiLeaks for publishing government secrets would set a dangerous precedent."[7]

With an increasing number of leaks to the press of sensitive material, many have questioned whether the press has too much freedom under the First Amendment. Is the release of classified information always a threat to national security? In some instances, does it make sense to keep information from the American public? In its role as government watchdog, is the press entitled to have access to the details of what the US government is involved in, even if the government wants to keep this information under wraps? These are the questions courts are grappling with as they work to find a balance between national security and Americans' right to know.

DISCUSSION STARTERS

- Should regulations guaranteeing net neutrality be rolled back? Why or why not?

- Do you think whistle-blowers should be prosecuted for leaking classified information? Why or why not?

- Does the press have too much freedom? Why or why not?

CHAPTER 8

THE FUTURE OF
PRESS FREEDOM

The world was riveted by the news after the 9/11 tragedy.

There is no doubt that freedom of the press has been adversely affected by the tightening of security since the 9/11 World Trade Center and Pentagon attacks in 2001. In court cases where journalists' access to information has been pitted against possible risks to national security, judges have decided in the interest of national security.

As a result, journalists have felt their freedoms are more restricted. Reporters, for instance, no longer believe their communication channels are secure. This especially rings true for those who have been researching stories

THE PATRIOT ACT

In the wake of the 9/11 terrorist attacks in 2001, the US government passed the USA Patriot Act in an attempt to crack down on those who may pose a threat to national security. Under the Material Support section of the Act, a journalist who interviews anyone connected to organizations on the terrorist list to gather information about a story could be sent to prison. This is a clear violation of First Amendment rights. The Patriot Act restricts First Amendment freedoms in other ways, too. According to the Reporters Committee for Freedom of the Press, the law allows the government to demand that reporters hand over their notes and possibly even force them to reveal sources. Beefed-up surveillance threatens communications between journalists and sources as well. Without a guarantee of confidentiality, some sources will not talk with journalists, limiting the amount of information reporters are able to gather.

about national security who have discovered that their e-mail and phone records have been reviewed without their consent.

While doing whatever can possibly be done to ensure that attacks of the magnitude of 9/11 never happen again is certainly necessary, the United States remains a democracy. In a democracy, checks and balances are still needed on all branches of government. As Sophia Cope, of the Newspaper Association of America, explains, the press still fulfills a valuable role. "A free press is very important to uncover what the government is doing and hold it accountable. To maintain balance between

The Free Flow of Information Act was introduced in 2007 by Senator Richard Lugar.

governmental power and the power of the citizenry, we need accountability reporting—arguably, particularly post-9/11."[1]

FREE FLOW OF INFORMATION ACT

Efforts to pass a federal Free Flow of Information Act, otherwise known as the shield law, are one attempt to reclaim a degree of press freedom for journalists. Shield laws protect journalists from having to reveal their sources. Although many states have shield laws of their own—some granting absolute privilege for sources and others having exceptions—a federal law has yet to pass both the House and Senate. The last time the bill was introduced was in 2013 when it was proposed by Senator Charles E. Schumer, a Democrat from New York. The bill passed in the Senate but never passed in the House.

Yet some critics of the bill argue that rather than limiting the instances when journalists will be asked to reveal sources, the Free Flow of Information Act actually places more limitations on press freedom, especially for smaller, independent news organizations. The bill defines *journalist* in a way that excludes those not in a union, guild, or on a regular payroll, such as freelancers and independent journalists. Major media companies are increasingly relying on reports by independent journalists

WHAT HAPPENS TO JOURNALISTS WHO REFUSE TO REVEAL SOURCES?

In 2005, former *New York Times* reporter Judith Miller spent 85 days in jail for refusing to break her promise of confidentiality and reveal her source.[2] Although she conducted interviews, Miller never actually wrote an article on CIA operative Valerie Plame, whose identity was revealed in a story by columnist Robert Novak. Miller told Judge Thomas F. Hogan, "If journalists cannot be trusted to guarantee confidentiality, then journalists cannot function and there cannot be a free press."[3] Judge Hogan replied, "I have a person in front of me who is defying the law."[4] He then sent her to jail. After serving jail time, Miller eventually testified.

to cut costs and keep journalists on the payroll out of harm's way. These growing numbers of independent journalists would not be covered under the Free Flow of Information Act. In addition, the bill allows judges to make final decisions as to what exactly threatens national security. These decisions may actually increase the likelihood that journalists will be forced to reveal their sources.

PRESIDENT VS. THE PRESS

So what does the future hold for freedom of the press? The early months of the Trump administration suggest that First Amendment rights will continue to face challenges.

Although many presidents have had strained relationships with the press in the past, President Trump came out swinging at the media on the campaign trail. Trump, a New York real estate mogul and celebrity in his own right, had plenty of experience dealing with the media through the years. As a presidential candidate, he often accused the media of spreading fake news and promised that if he were elected president, he would hold the press accountable for accurately reporting the news.

Trump didn't waste any time in keeping his promise. On January 21, 2017, the day after President Trump's inauguration, his administration called out the press for spreading false

President Trump talking about "fake" news in January 2017

news by underreporting the size of Trump's Inauguration Day crowd. The administration stated it would "hold the press accountable."[5]

At first glance, this seems like a somewhat silly argument. What difference does it make how many people attended a presidential inauguration? But it established a pattern that would become very familiar to the American people: the Trump administration calling out the media for not getting its facts straight and identifying the news from some sources—mainly those that paint the Trump administration in a negative light—as "fake" news. Placing the label "fake" on certain news sources and journalists plants the seed that the media can't be trusted or that it is lying to the American people. With each accusation of spreading fake news, the Trump administration added a dent in the media's credibility with the nation.

If the media is not to be trusted, who is? And what happens to the media's role as the government watchdog? So began a back-and-forth battle between the president and the media that would dominate President Trump's first few months in office. The president claimed the press was not telling

AMERICAN PUBLIC: CAN'T WE ALL JUST GET ALONG?

It's clear that the media and President Trump are at odds with each other. But what do the American people think? In a poll conducted by the Pew Research Center, American citizens revealed that they don't like the antagonistic relationship between President Trump and the press. In fact, 83 percent of those polled thought the relationship between Trump and the media is unhealthy. Another 73 percent thought that their poor relationship was interfering with access to news that matters. Other polls have indicated that those who align with Trump are far more likely to distrust the media than Democrats.[6]

the truth, whereas the media claimed Trump was avoiding the truth.

The American Civil Liberties Union's Executive Director Anthony D. Romero offered the following reaction: "It is shameful that on the first full day of this administration, we have ominous suggestions of possible government censorship. . . . This will be a fight the Trump administration will most certainly lose. If Trump wants to take on the First Amendment, we will see him in court."[7]

REPORTING CLASSIFIED INFORMATION

In May 2017, the media reacted in alarm to an order issued by President Trump after FBI director James Comey was fired by the Trump administration. Shortly after he was fired, Comey revealed that on February 14 Trump told Comey that he should begin arresting journalists who publish classified information.

Bruce Brown, executive director of the Reporter's Committee for Freedom of the Press, responded, "The comments attributed to President Trump cross a dangerous line. But no president gets to jail journalists. Reporters are protected by judges and juries, by a congress that relies on them to stay informed, and by a Justice Department that for decades has honored the role of a free press by spurning prosecutions of journalists for publishing leaks of classified information."[8]

Martin Baron, executive editor for the *Washington Post*, took Trump's words as a threat: "Suggesting that the government should prosecute journalists for the publication of classified information is very menacing, and I think that's exactly what they intend. It's an act of intimidation."[9]

The idea of throwing journalists in jail for publishing classified information brings up thoughts of how journalists are treated in nations without First Amendment rights that guarantee freedom of the press. These places include Turkey, where 120 journalists have been jailed since a failed attempt to overthrow the government in July 2016, and Mexico, where 104 or more journalists have been murdered and 25 have gone missing in recent years. In Russia, reporters are routinely threatened, hurt, killed, or thrown in prison by the government.

Is the publication of classified information considered a First Amendment right? Some claim that if the information is of interest to the public, it should be covered under First Amendment freedoms. Others believe it depends on how the classified information was obtained. For example, if the journalist broke laws by wiretapping to get the information, it should not be protected under the First Amendment.

During times of war, of course, different rules apply. Some claim the United States has been at war—the war on terror—since 9/11, and publication of classified information could be considered a threat to national security. All is open to future interpretation, ultimately by Supreme Court justices.

President Trump has called the media "enemies of the people," a phrase also used by Communist leader Joseph Stalin.[10] Although Trump later clarified that he was referring to "fake news" as an enemy of the

PRESIDENT SKIPS PRESS CORRESPONDENTS' DINNER

In April 2017, President Trump decided to skip the annual Press Correspondents' Association Dinner, an event US presidents have attended consistently for years. In fact, this was the first time since 1981 that the media dined without the president— President Ronald Reagan didn't attend because he had just been shot. The dinner, in which the president, members of the press, and Hollywood celebrities meet, greet, and poke fun at each other, is traditionally a night when the press and the president establish some sort of rapport. Many were not at all surprised the president refused to attend, citing the difficult relationship between Trump and the press. But journalists and celebrities rallied, turning the event into a pep rally of sorts for the press. Journalists recited the First Amendment and declared that the news is not fake and they are not an enemy of the people. Meanwhile, Trump held a campaign rally in Pennsylvania, where he continued to criticize fake news reported by the media.

No matter who is president, journalists will continue to serve as watchdogs and inform American citizens on what's happening behind the scenes with the US government.

people, such comments suggest that the president does not believe the media's role as government watchdog is important to the democratic process. The Trump administration has pledged to "do something about" the fact that journalists are allowed to use anonymous sources.[11] President Trump has also promised to rework libel laws so that people can sue the media more easily for publishing inaccurate or harmful information about them. These developments point decidedly toward greater scrutiny of the boundaries of freedom of the press in the years to come.

DISCUSSION STARTERS

- Is arresting journalists justified if the information they print is classified?

- How would forcing journalists to reveal their sources jeopardize freedom of the press?

- Is there such a thing as "fake" news? What do you think President Trump means when he uses this term?

TIMELINE

1639

Printing is introduced in the American colonies in Cambridge, Massachusetts.

1735

New York Weekly Journal printer John Peter Zenger is sued for publishing critical stories about public officials. The ruling is overturned, because the stories were true.

1791

The First Amendment is adopted by the US government, with the goal of preventing the government from censoring the press.

1801

Thomas Jefferson takes office and pardons those arrested under the Sedition Act. The Supreme Court eventually overturns the act, claiming it violates freedom of the press.

1804

Alexander Hamilton defends *Wasp* newspaper editor Harry Croswell in a libel case.

1861–1865

During the Civil War, more than 300 newspapers are shut down for publishing stories that oppose the war. Newspaper editors are thrown in jail for being disloyal to the North.

1931

In *Near v. Minnesota*, the Supreme Court rules that the First Amendment prohibits the government from using prior restraints. Almost all forms of restraint on free speech are declared unconstitutional.

1964

In *New York Times Co. v. Sullivan*, the Supreme Court rules that newspapers are protected from lawsuits when they print information that is incorrect but do not know it at the time and intent is not malicious.

1968

Negative press coverage of the Vietnam War on TV plays a part in turning the American public against the war.

1971

The Pentagon Papers, classified documents on US involvement in the Vietnam War, are released to the public.

1972

On June 17, 1972, five men affiliated with the Nixon reelection campaign break into the Watergate office building and attempt to bug the DNC headquarters. *Washington Post* reporters Bob Woodward and Carl Bernstein break the story.

2001

After the 9/11 attacks, the US government passes the Patriot Act, allowing it to investigate those who may pose a threat to national security. Personal civil liberties, including those related to freedom of the press, are on the line.

2006

Julian Assange launches WikiLeaks, with the mission to publish original documents of "political, ethical, diplomatic, or historical" significance, provided by anonymous sources.

2013

Edward Snowden, a contractor for the NSA, leaks information to the press (the *Guardian*) about surveillance the US government was conducting on US citizens. Snowden is granted asylum in Russia.

2017

The Trump administration accuses the press of reporting fake news and says the administration will hold the press accountable. President Trump calls the media "enemies of the people." It is revealed that on February 14, Trump told former FBI director James Comey that he should begin arresting journalists who publish classified information.

ESSENTIAL FACTS

FREEDOM OF THE PRESS

The First Amendment to the Constitution guarantees five freedoms: of religion, speech, the press, and assembly, and to petition the government for a redress of grievances. The Amendment reads, "Congress shall make no law . . . abridging the freedom of speech, or of the press."

LIMITATIONS

The following limitations are placed on press freedom:

- Offensive sexual material is not protected by the First Amendment because courts argue it has no value to society.

- Anything that threatens national security is not protected by the First Amendment.

- In times of war, the press cannot publish details about troop locations, plans to attack, or similar information that threatens the war effort.

KEY PLAYERS

- Julian Assange is a computer programmer who founded the Internet news organization WikiLeaks in 2006.

- Carl Bernstein and Bob Woodward are former investigative reporters for the *Washington Post* who worked to report the Watergate scandal, which eventually led to President Richard Nixon's resignation.

- Walter Cronkite was a well-regarded television news reporter whose broadcasts and commentary after the Tet Offensive in 1968 shifted American opinion of US involvement in the Vietnam War.

- Andrew Hamilton was a trial lawyer who represented John Peter Zenger in 1735 in the first libel case in colonial America. His argument was: if it's true, it can't be libel.

- Thomas Jefferson was a Founding Father and president of the United States who defended and supported freedom of the press.
- James Madison was a Founding Father and author of the First Amendment to the Constitution.
- Judith Miller is a former reporter for the *New York Times* who went to jail in 2005 for refusing to reveal a source.
- John Peter Zenger was a publisher of the *New York Weekly Journal* who was arrested and went to court in 1735 for printing defamatory articles about Governor William Crosby.

KEY PERSPECTIVES

The purpose of the media is to act as a watchdog of the government. In this role, the media is a fourth branch of the government, providing checks and balances on the executive, legislative, and judicial branches.

- Thomas Jefferson felt that without a free press, democracy suffers.
- In the past, some news leaks have posed a threat to national security.
- In times of war, freedom of the press is restricted to protect national security.
- Freedom of the press has relied on the help of confidential sources.
- Journalists are held accountable for errors in reporting.

QUOTE

"Were it left to me to decide whether we should have a government without newspapers or newspapers without government, I should not hesitate for a moment to prefer the latter."

— *Thomas Jefferson, 1787*

GLOSSARY

BIAS
Prejudice in favor of or against one thing, person, or group compared with another, usually in a way considered to be unfair.

CENSORSHIP
The act of imposing values on others by limiting what they may read, write, hear, or see.

DEFAMATORY
False and intended to harm a person's reputation.

DISSEMINATE
To spread information widely.

GAG ORDER
A court-issued restraint that forbids the press from covering a court case.

IMPEACH
To charge an elected official with wrongdoing.

INVESTIGATIVE REPORTER
A journalist who digs deep into a topic, such as a crime, corruption, or wrongdoing, and writes articles about the discoveries.

LEAK
To give classified information to the media.

LIBEL
A published false statement that is damaging to a person's reputation.

MARTIAL LAW
When the military takes control of a country or part of a country.

OBSTRUCTION OF JUSTICE
Attempts to hide information or details that are essential to a criminal investigation.

PARTISAN
Strongly divided by political party with a general refusal to compromise.

PRIOR RESTRAINT
A government's attempt to prevent publication of news.

SEDITION LAWS
Laws that make it illegal for someone to write or speak out against the government.

SUBPOENAED
Called to testify in court as a witness.

TREASON
The crime of betraying one's country.

WATCHDOG
The role of a free press in a democracy, which is to watch over all branches of government and speak up when one of these branches is violating the Constitution.

WHISTLE-BLOWER
A person who informs authorities about an individual or institution he or she thinks is involved in illegal activity.

ADDITIONAL RESOURCES

SELECTED BIBLIOGRAPHY

Bollinger, Lee C. *Uninhibited, Robust, and Wide-Open: A Free Press for a New Century*. New York: Oxford UP, 2010. Print.

Silva, Cristina. "How Alexander Hamilton Helped Create a Free Press, and the Libel Laws Trump Wants to Tear Down." *Newsweek*. Newsweek, 1 May 2017. Web. 19 May 2017.

Slack, Charles. *Liberty's First Crisis: Adams, Jefferson, and the Misfits Who Saved Free Speech*. New York: Atlantic Monthly, 2015. Print.

FURTHER READINGS

Archer, Jules. *Watergate: A Story of Richard Nixon and the Shocking 1972 Scandal*. New York, NY: Sky Pony, 2015. Print.

Bodden, Valerie. *Muckrakers: Ida Tarbell Takes on Big Business*. Minneapolis, MN: Abdo, 2017. Print.

Rouff, Ruth. *Ida B. Wells: A Woman of Courage*. West Berlin, NJ: Townsend, 2010. Print.

ONLINE RESOURCES

Booklinks
NONFICTION NETWORK
FREE! ONLINE NONFICTION RESOURCES

To learn more about freedom of the press, visit **abdobooklinks.com**. These links are routinely monitored and updated to provide the most current information available.

MORE INFORMATION

For more information on this subject, contact or visit the following organizations:

FEDERAL HALL NATIONAL MEMORIAL NEW YORK

26 Wall Street
New York, NY 10005
212-825-6990

nps.gov/feha/index.htm

Visit the New York City courtroom where Andrew Hamilton defended the rights of John Peter Zenger in the first libel case.

NEWSEUM

555 Pennsylvania Avenue NW
Washington, DC 20001
202-292-6100

newseum.org/visit

A museum dedicated to defending freedom of expression and the five freedoms of the First Amendment, the Newseum features exhibits and programs that showcase the history of the media.

SOURCE NOTES

CHAPTER 1. WATERGATE

1. Jim Hunt and Bob Risch. *Warrior: Frank Sturgis—The CIA's #1 Assassin-Spy, Who Nearly Killed Castro but Was Ambushed by Watergate*. New York: Tor Books, 2012. Print. 138.

2. Karlyn Barker and Walter Pincus. "Watergate Revisited: 20 Years after the Break-in, the Story Continues to Unfold." *Washington Post*. Washington Post, 14 June 1992. Web. 14 Sept. 2017.

3. "The Watergate Story." *Washington Post*. Washington Post, n.d. Web. 14 Sept. 2017.

4. Ibid.

5. Carl Bernstein and Bob Woodward. "Woodward and Bernstein: 40 Years after Watergate, Nixon Was Far Worse Than We Thought." *Washington Post*. Washington Post, 8 June 2012. Web. 14 Sept. 2017.

6. Sara James. "Watergate Proved Freedom of the Press Vital to Safeguard Democracy." *Courier-Mail*. Courier-Mail, 29 July 2014. Web. 14 Sept. 2017.

CHAPTER 2. A ROCKY START FOR FREEDOM

1. "Freedom of the Press." *Supreme Court Drama: Cases That Changed America*. *Gale*. Gale Cengage Learning, n.d. Web. 14 Sept. 2017.

2. "The Trial of John Peter Zenger." *US History*. Independence Hall Association in Philadelphia, n.d. Web. 14 Sept. 2017.

3. "John Madison's Contribution to the Constitution." *America's Library*. Library of Congress, n.d. Web. 14 Sept. 2017.

4. Lindsey Bever. "Memo to Donald Trump: Thomas Jefferson Invented Hating the Media." *Washington Post*. Washington Post, 17 Feb. 2017. Web. 14 Sept. 2017.

5. Ibid.

CHAPTER 3. TIMES OF WAR

1. Geoffrey R. Stone. "Freedom of the Press in Time of War." *Chicago Unbound*. University of Chicago Law School, 2006. Web. 14 Sept. 2017.

2. "Civil War Tested Lincoln's Tolerance for Free Speech, Press." *First Amendment Center*. First Amendment Center, 11 Feb. 2009. Web. 14 Sept. 2017.

3. Geoffrey R. Stone. "Freedom of the Press in Time of War." *Chicago Unbound*. University of Chicago Law School, 2006. Web. 14 Sept. 2017.

4. "Civil War Tested Lincoln's Tolerance for Free Speech, Press." *First Amendment Center*. First Amendment Center, 11 Feb. 2009. Web. 14 Sept. 2017.

5. "1916 Election." *Woodrow Wilson House*. The President Woodrow Wilson House, n.d. Web. 14 Sept. 2017.

6. Geoffrey R. Stone. "Freedom of the Press in Time of War." *Chicago Unbound*. University of Chicago Law School, 2006. Web. 14 Sept. 2017.

7. Ibid.

8. "A 'Clear and Present Danger.'" *Constitutional Rights Foundation*. Constitutional Rights Foundation, n.d. Web. 14 Sept. 2017.

9. Ibid.

CHAPTER 4. VIETNAM WAR IN THE LIVING ROOM

1. "War and the Media: Press Freedom vs. Military Censorship." *Constitutional Rights Foundation*. Constitutional Rights Foundation, n.d. Web. 14 Sept. 2017.

2. "Learning from the Civil Rights during Vietnam Era." *San Diego African American Museum of Fine Arts*. San Diego African American Museum of Fine Arts, 10 Nov. 2016. Web. 14 Sept. 2017.

3. "The Impact Journalism Had on the Vietnam War." *History and Journalism*. History and Journalism, n.d. Web. 14 Sept. 2017.

4. Marilyn B. Young and Robert Buzzanco. *A Companion to the Vietnam War*. Hoboken, NJ: Wiley-Blackwell. Print. 454.

5. "War and the Media: Press Freedom vs. Military Censorship." *Constitutional Rights Foundation*. Constitutional Rights Foundation, n.d. Web. 14 Sept. 2017.

6. Ibid.

7. "Vietnam and TV News." *Dawn of the Eye: The History of Television*. Canadian Broadcasting Company, 27 Apr. 2011. Web. 26 May 2017.

8. "Final Words: Cronkite's Vietnam Commentary." *NPR*. NPR, 18 July 2009. Web. 14 Sept. 2017.

9. Leslie Clark. "About Walter Cronkite." *PBS*. Public Broadcasting Service, 26 July 2006. Web. 14 Sept. 2017.

10. "War and the Media: Press Freedom vs. Military Censorship." *Constitutional Rights Foundation*. Constitutional Rights Foundation, n.d. Web. 14 Sept. 2017.

SOURCE NOTES CONTINUED

CHAPTER 5. CENSORSHIP AND PRIOR RESTRAINT

1. "Government Censorship (Prior Restraints)." *Reporters Committee for Freedom of the Press*. Reporters Committee for Freedom of the Press, n.d. Web. 14 Sept. 2017.

2. "Near v. Minnesota ex rel. Olson." *Oyez*. Legal Information Institute, Cornell Law School, Justia, IIT Chicago-Kent College of Law, n.d. Web. 14 Sept. 2017.

3. Thomas I. Emerson. "The Doctrine of Prior Restraint." *Yale Law School Digital Commons*. Yale Law School Legal Scholarship Repository, n.d. Web. 14 Sept. 2017.

4. "Lovell v. City of Griffin." *Justia*. Justia US Supreme Court, n.d. Web. 14 Sept. 2017.

CHAPTER 6. LIBEL

1. "Advertisement, 'Heed Their Rising Voices,' New York Times, May 29, 1960." *Archives*. National Archives, n.d. Web. 14 Sept. 2017.

2. Cristina Silva. "How Alexander Hamilton Helped Create a Free Press, and the Libel Laws Trump Wants to Tear Down." *Newsweek*. Newsweek, 1 May 2017. Web. 14 Sept. 2017.

3. "New York Times v. Sullivan." *Bill of Rights Institute*. Bill of Rights Institute, n.d. Web. 14 Sept. 2017.

4. "Donald Trump vs. a Free Press." *New York Times*. New York Times, 13 Oct. 2016. Web. 14 Sept. 2017.

5. Hadas Gold. "Donald Trump: We're Going to 'Open Up' Libel Laws." *Politico*. Politico, 26 Feb. 2016. Web. 14 Sept. 2017.

6. "'Kato' Kaelin Settles Libel Suit with Tabloid." *Los Angeles Times*. Los Angeles Times, 9 Oct. 1999. Web. 14 Sept. 2017.

7. "Kaelin v. Globe Communications Corporation." *Find Law*. Thomson Reuters, n.d. Web. 14 Sept. 2017.

8. Hadas Gold. "Donald Trump: We're Going to 'Open Up' Libel Laws." *Politico*. Politico, 26 Feb. 2016. Web. 14 Sept. 2017.

CHAPTER 7. FREEDOM OF THE PRESS AND THE INTERNET

1. Michael Barthel. "5 Key Takeaways about the State of the News Media in 2016." *Pew Research Center*. Pew Research Center, 15 June 2016. Web. 14 Sept. 2017.

2. Elisa Shearer and Jeffrey Gottfried. "News Use Across Social Media Platforms 2017." *Pew Research Center*. Pew Research Center, 7 Sept. 2017. Web. 2 Oct. 2017.

3. "Lovell v. City of Griffin." *Justia*. Justia US Supreme Court, n.d. Web. 14 Sept. 2017.

4. Jonathan Zittrain and Molley Sauter. "Everything You Need to Know about WikiLeaks." *MIT Technology Review*. MIT Technology Review, 9 Dec. 2010. Web. 14 Sept. 2017.

5. Jane Onyanga-Omara and Tom Vanden Brook. "Chelsea Manning, Who Leaked 700,000 Documents to WikiLeaks, Released from Prison." *USA Today*. USA Today, 17 May 2017. Web. 14 Sept. 2017.

6. "Edward Snowden: Leaks That Exposed US Spy Programme." *BBC*. BBC, 17 Jan. 2014. Web. 14 Sept. 2017.

7. Mathew Ingram. "Why Charging WikiLeaks with Espionage Would Threaten a Free Press." *Fortune*. TIme, Inc., 21 Apr. 2017. Web. 14 Sept. 2017.

CHAPTER 8. THE FUTURE OF PRESS FREEDOM

1. Anna Stolley Persky. "50 Years after New York Times v. Sullivan, Do Courts Still Value Journalists' Watchdog Role?" *ABA Journal*. American Bar Association, 1 Mar. 2014. Web. 14 Sept. 2017.

2. Ibid.

3. Adam Liptak. "Reporter Jailed after Refusing to Name Source." *New York Times*. New York Times, 7 July 2005. Web. 14 Sept. 2017.

4. Ibid.

5. "ACLU: Spicer Comments on Media Ring of McCarthyism, Will Lead to Losing Legal Battles." *ACLU*. American Civil Liberties Union, 21 Jan. 2017. Web. 14 Sept. 2017.

6. Noah Bierman. "President Trump and the Media Are Feuding. The Public Isn't Happy." *Los Angeles Times*. Los Angeles Times, 4 Apr. 2017. Web. 14 Sept. 2017.

7. "ACLU: Spicer Comments on Media Ring of McCarthyism, Will Lead to Losing Legal Battles." *ACLU*. American Civil Liberties Union, 21 Jan. 2017. Web. 14 Sept. 2017.

8. Michael Walsh. "The Comey Memo Was Also about Trump's Request to Arrest Reporters. Journalists Call It 'Crazy and Scary.'" *Yahoo*. Yahoo News, 17 May 2017. Web. 14 Sept. 2017.

9. Michael M. Grynbaum, Sydney Ember, and Charlie Savage. "Trump's Urging That Comey Jail Reporters Denounced as an 'Act of Intimidation.'" *New York Times*. New York Times, 17 May 2017. Web. 14 Sept. 2017.

10. Michael J. Abramowitz. "Hobbling a Champion of Global Press Freedom." *Freedom House*. Freedom House, n.d. Web. 14 Sept. 2017.

11. David Jackson. "Trump Again Calls Media 'Enemy of the People.'" *USA Today*. USA Today, 24 Feb. 2017. Web. 14 Sept. 2017.

INDEX

M

Madison, James, 22, 26–27, 51
Manning, Chelsea, 80–82
McNamara, Robert, 56–57

N

Near v. Minnesota, 53
Nebraska Press Association v. Stuart, 61
net neutrality, 77–79
New York Times, 58–60, 63, 65, 66, 67, 88
New York Times Co. v. Sullivan, 63, 67, 72
Nixon, Richard, 8–14, 58

O

Obama, Barack, 78

P

Pentagon Papers, 56–60
prior restraint, 22, 51–52, 54–56, 58, 60

R

Revolutionary War, 29

S

Schenck, Charles, 36
Sedition Act, 24, 26–27, 36
Snowden, Edward, 82
Sullivan, L. B., 64–65
Supreme Court, 19, 27, 30, 36–37, 52–56, 58, 60–61, 63, 65, 67, 77, 95

T

television, 15, 43–44, 47, 49, 76
Tet Offensive, 47, 59
Truman, Harry, 57
Trump, Donald, 71–72, 78, 89–95, 97

V

Vietcong, 9, 45, 47
Vietnam War, 9, 39–40, 42–47, 49, 56–58, 59, 73

W

Washington Post, 7, 10, 58, 60, 82, 94
Watergate, 5–8, 10–15, 73
Wells-Barnett, Ida, 32
Wilson, Woodrow, 34–35
Woodward, Bob, 7–8, 10, 14
World War I, 32, 34–36, 39
World War II, 34, 39

Z

Zeigler, Ronald, 6
Zenger, John Peter, 19–21

ABOUT THE AUTHORS

DUCHESS HARRIS, JD, PHD

Professor Harris is the chair of the American Studies Department at Macalester College. The author and coauthor of four books (*Hidden Human Computers: The Black Women of NASA* and *Black Lives Matter* with Sue Bradford Edwards, *Racially Writing the Republic: Racists, Race Rebels, and Transformations of American Identity* with Bruce Baum, and *Black Feminist Politics from Kennedy to Clinton/Obama*), she has been an associate editor for *Litigation News*, the American Bar Association Section's quarterly flagship publication, and was the first editor-in-chief of *Law Raza Journal*, an interactive online race and the law journal for William Mitchell College of Law.

She has earned a PhD in American Studies from the University of Minnesota and a Juris Doctorate from William Mitchell College of Law.

KARI A. CORNELL

Kari Cornell is a writer and editor who loves to read, garden, cook, run, and craft. She is the author of the award winning book, *The Nitty-Gritty Gardening Book: Fun Projects for All Seasons*, and many other histories, biographies, and cookbooks for kids. She lives in Minneapolis, Minnesota, with her husband, two sons, and her crazy dog, Emmylou.